The Way I See It

The Way I See It

THE POETRY OF
ANNE NEWMAN

BANKHOUSE

First published in the UK in 2019 by
Bank House Books

ISBN 9780993349454

Original photography
Anne Newman
Author portraits
Della Newman
Production, layout and design:
Dave Randle

Foreword

This book has been compiled over a number of years. I would have completed it much earlier, but life always seemed to get in the way. But that, I think has added to the depth of life's ups and downs, happy and sad.

If you don't have the difficult times, you cannot appreciate the good ones. We all, I think, see life differently through older eyes!

My poems have materialised mainly from watching nature, life, and people. They have included my own experiences, (often exaggerated in some of them in order to enable them to rhyme!)

Many of the serious poems in this book have often been written through tears of emotion, but I have included these so that you, my reader, can perhaps, relate to them through your own life experiences.

The world has changed tremendously since my own childhood days, some of it for the better, some for the worse. We can never change this world alone, but by our individual thoughts, 'words' and deeds we can make it a better place for future generations.

I hope you will enjoy reading this book as much as I have enjoyed writing it!

Dedication.

I dedicate this book to my husband for his continued patience in waiting for meals!

Also my son and daughter for always choosing their 'words' carefully!

To all the friends, (you know who you are!) who have supported and encouraged me throughout.

Contents

The Wonder of the Written Word   1
Mornin' Campers   2
The Procedure   3
The Plight of the Humble Gardener   4
Bluebells   5
Seeing Fairies
Happy Hollyhocks   6
The Little People   7
Just
The Fairy Ring   8
The Open Gate
The Field of Lavender   9
The Great British Barbecue   10
The Last Rose of Summer   12
The Sailing Dream
I always Meant to Tell You   13
Before the Storm   14
Just a Face in the Crowd   15
If Only   16
When All the Fun Stopped   17
Sleep Walk   18
Following the Plough   19
Stitches of Patience   20
The Button Tin   21
SAT-NAV Insanity   22
Winter's Cold Embrace   23
Cottage by the Sea   24
All in a Heartbeat   25
Echoes on the Stairway   26
Hopes and Dreams   27
Streets, Walls and Secrets   28
The Memory Book   29
The Tale of the Lonely Shopping-Trolley   30
Just a House   31
Daisy Chains   32
The Street at Night
Promise of Life   33
When the Tide Comes Rolling In   34
The Weight Watcher   35

The Sea Shore   36
The Mask I Wear   37
The Lonely Road   38
Dry Stone Wall   39
Simple Deeds   40
The Dreaded Takeaway   41
When Somebody Cares   42
When the Piano Ceased to Play
Shopping Mall   43
It's All in my Mind   44
Dance of the Swallows   45
I Heard an Organ Play
Which Way do you Hang Your Toilet Roll?   46
Nothing in Life is for Certain   48
Live in Hope   50
Train Ride   51
I'm Nobody's Fool   52
I kow I've put it Somewhere   53
Away from it All   54
The 'Wind' of Change   55
A Photograph of Grandma   56
Carousel   57
Chasing Shadows
A Picture Painted in Words   59
The Legacy in the Leaves   60
At Life's Helm   61
Winter's Angels   62
Ted's Beloved Greenhouse   63
Up on the Moors   64
Only a Tree   65
The 'One' who Holds the Moon   66

About the Author   68

The Wonder of the Written Word.

The pen touches the paper,
The ink begins to flow.
I see the words within my mind,
I feel the excitement grow.

I never know quite where to start,
I listen to my beating heart,
And then, imagination grows,
And steadily a sentence flows!

Then, in a while, I have a rhyme,
It may have taken quite some time.
Sometimes it grows with speed and glory,
And almost turns into a story!

These thoughts emerge quite eerily,
From things I've seen and heard.
I'm fortunate that I have found
The wonder of the written word!!

Mornin' Campers.

The rain doth fall, the wind is blowing,
And here I sit, my canvas sewing.
'Why am I here?' I ask myself,
'I started off with mirth and stealth.'

Things don't look good this morning,
And we're looking all forlorn
As we hammer down our tent pegs
To the onslaught of the storm.

The weather men are full of doom and dread
They say that there are gloomy times ahead.
But us ardent' campers, on we must!
Erecting tents in mud or dust.
In our designer boots and 'North Face' clothing,
When all the while, the weather we are loathing!

I hear a 'crack' and then a 'blast'...
Was that a tent I saw fly past?
Surely the wind cannot uproot a tent so fine?
I pray it will not do the same to mine.

As the torch begins to fade, and we batten down the hatches,
Retrieve the candles from the bag ...but forgot to pack the matches!
We cuddle down together saying, 'This can't last all night.'
And then another clap of thunder makes us realise our plight!
The rain comes down like stair-rods and the tent poles start to bow
We've nearly lost the will to live, but mustn't get too low.

As we awake another day, the rain is set to fall
There's word the bottom field's awash, have mercy on us all!
For that's our only exit and we're due to leave tomorrow
It looks as if our holiday is doomed to give us sorrow!

But camping CAN be so much fun and we know we'll come again,
To 'endure' such happy memories ... of wind and mud, and rain!
We know for sure when we have packed up all our gear
And we're on our homeward run,
The clouds will swiftly disappear from view ...
And out will come the SUN!

The Plight of the Humble Gardener.

Here I sit, full of woe, with devastation high and low.
The moles have tunnelled in the turf, and shifted several tons of earth.
The little bastards are a pain, my lawn wont be the same again.
The greenfly have invaded, the blackfly are as bad,
They've sucked my climbing plants to death and I'm feeling rather sad.
The slugs and snails have left their slime on everything I've grown,
They've munched their way through countless plants,
They make me want to moan.
My pots have been invaded by the Wireworm and the Weevil,
I'm usually quite placid, but today I'm feeling evil.
The wind we had the other day has burned my Acer tree,
And my Lupin's leaning over at a worrying degree!!
I've spent a fortune lately on bedding plants and such,
But next doors cat has dug them out (he doesn't care too much.)
In fact, as if for spite, he's scented all around,
So that cats will come from miles away to 'shite' upon my ground!!
The Pigeons have decapitated all my runner beans,
And they sit there 'smirking' on the fence . . . .
(Until they start upon my greens!!)
The Bindweed's strangled all in sight, it really is a pain,
I dig it out, and then it's back and strangling all again!
So, armed with pesticides and pellets, and shot gun underarm,
I shall conquer all the 'critters' which have caused my plants such harm.
I'll hope for peace upon my plot and better days ahead,
Then I'll sit and read my 'Gardeners News'
Whilst relaxing in my shed!!

The 'Procedure' (Colonoscopy.)

I've taken the prescribed liquid, which I didn't really like,
And it's had me on the toilet for the best part of last night!

I've got my hospital gown on, it's open at the rear,
I've done a bit of 'side-stepping' in case anyone should peer!

I'm feeling rather nervous, as I know what to expect.
I've read the given leaflet, and had time to reflect.

But now I have to take the plunge, the consent form has been signed,
And as I move towards the bed, I'm feeling less inclined!

They've pumped me full of oxygen, to help them with their plight,
They say I'll have some 'flatulence' today and half the night!

The surgeon has his gloves on, and his mask is now in place,
I suspect he has a crafty little 'smirk' upon his face!

You see, he does this every day, he doesn't sense my fear,
I bet he's never ever had a camera up his rear!!

He says "Relax" I grit my teeth, the nurse's hand I hold,
I need to focus hard and do the things I have been told.

I feel a queer sensation and I glance up at the screen,
I get a glimpse of all the places I have never seen!!

I won't go into detail. But when the 'deed' is done,
I slink into the cubicle and I feel quite overcome!

Relief is what I'm feeling after all that 'pent up' dread
For a necessary 'procedure' on a hard old hospital bed!

Now to wait for positive results, I can hardly stand the strain,
I do not feel the urge to have that 'procedure' EVER again!

Seeing Fairies?

I saw a fairy in a glade,
She looked right back at me.
I gazed at her in wonderment
As she sat beneath a tree.
Around her dainty silhouette
There shone the brightest hue.
Her wings all glittered, gossamer
As they caught the morning dew.
I gloried in that moment
For I felt that time stood still.
All around me there was silence,
And I felt an eerie chill.
I glanced away for just a second,
When I looked back, she had gone.
Was it my imagination . . . .
Or was I the chosen one?

Bluebells.

Standing in this silent place
Far away from human race.
Observing every living thing
Swaying branches, birds that sing.

There's nothing that is quite so grand
As fragrant bluebells close at hand.
Inhale the scent that's all around
And thank the Lord for all you've found.

Happy Hollyhocks.

What a colourful sight to see,
Attracting butterfly and bee.
Petals fluttering in the breeze,
Happy moments watching these.
Amazing shades, all standing proud,
Saying, "Look at me and my happy crowd!"
Adorable, soft pastel-coloured Hollyhocks,
Frivolous flowers with frilly frocks!

The Little People.

When everyone is fast asleep,
The little people, out they creep.
They dance and sing beneath the moon
But nobody hears their lilting tune.
Only believers of fairy world
Will see this spectacle unfurled.
They fill the place with happy sound,
And leave their magic all around!

Just.

Just a sandy beach and sky,
Just the birds that sing on high.
Just the sun that shines so bright,
Just the moon and stars at night.
Just a place, not far away,
Just a place I'd like to stay.

The Fairy Ring.

I heard a sweet and mellow sound
That drifted on the breeze,
And then I saw the fairies
Dancing gracefully by the trees.
I stepped closer so that I could gaze
Upon this glorious sight,
But at that moment, they disappeared
Into the dew filled night.

The Open Gate.

The light shines through the open gate,
Will you go through, or will you wait?
You feel the 'pull' of the unknown,
Is someone there, am I alone?
If I go through, can I get back?
Give me the courage that I lack.
Decisions face us every day,
We cannot always walk away . . .

The Field of Lavender.

The day was warm, the sky was blue,
I stood there, transfixed by the view.
The aroma was so pungent,
It took my breathe away,
All around was Lavender
On that glorious sunny day.

Furrow upon furrow,
Flowers swaying in the breeze,
The bluest haze of loveliness
Like the movement of the sea.

I won't forget that moment
As I stood there in a trance . . . .
I'll be going back again one day,
To that fragrant field in France.

The Great British Barbecue

Here we sit on plastic chairs, the sun is shining bright,
The wood we used was soaking wet, so the charcoal wouldn't light!
Ah! Now the coals are burning, there's hope for all who wait . .
(Dad had to use some panels from the garden gate!)

I feel quite optimistic, now the heavy smoke is clearing,
The meat is sizzling nicely and the guests have started cheering.
They know that it is imminent that there'll be some food tonight,
They're queuing now quite briskly, I hope there's not a fight!

The pasta's going down quite well and the salad's nearly gone,
Someone's suggested a cup of tea, I'll put the kettle on!
Those chops look very tasty, and that bit of steak . . . .
That reminds me, has anyone seen next door's tabby cat of late??!!

It seems the food is quite a hit, They've filled their plates again,
I'd better go and top things up . . . was that a spit of rain?
Thank God for the Gazebo, as it's raining now, quite hard,
The paper plates and serviettes took flight to next doors yard,
As now the wind has strengthened and the sky looks rather heavy,
But that hasn't stopped the guests from 'sinking' yet another 'Bevy'!!

They've all bought their rain macs, as they've learnt from past events,
Look!! Some have really got a cheek, they're setting up their tents!!
There's lightning now, and thunder, and great big hail-stones lay,
The lawn is under water, should we now call it a day?

The wind took the Gazebo, it crashed with such a thud,
And now the strawberry trifle is all trodden in the mud!

Our guests are saying their goodbyes, they know it's not worth staying,
They've had their fill, and some are ill, so there is no delaying!

So now it's time to clear the mess, and the sun's come out again,
The garden looks like a bombsite after all that rain.
We look, and feel bedraggled, I think we'll have a beer . . . .
I think we'll opt out of doing the barbecue next year!!

The Sailing Dream.

I made a little paper boat,
And on the pond I let it float.
I had great hopes to see it sail
But the wind blew hard, and my boat flailed.
It sunk and disappeared from view
And there was nothing I could do.

Sometimes in life, our dreams are lost,
Our thoughts upon the water tossed.
But we shall rise and steer our boat
To a place where it will safely float.
And we shall find our dreams once more . . .
On a distant, peaceful, far off shore.

Last Rose of Summer.

The last rose of Summer, it slowly will fade,
As frosty cold mornings, its petals invade.
The memory of its beauty will linger with you
As you think of its petals all covered with dew.
The fragrance, the colour, your spirit would lift,
The wonders of nature, a wonderful gift.
But now it is destined to shrivel and die,
As another harsh Winter passes you by.
But next year, God willing
There will be more,
To bring you this miracle
Just the same as before!

I always meant to tell you
(A poem dedicated to my parents)

Did I ever thank you for the things you done for me?
The sacrifices that you made, which I would never see.
The outings that you took me on, which you could least afford,
The times that you would cheer me up whenever I was bored.
The tales that you would tell me, about the 'olden times'
When you and Dad were in the war, and endless funny
rhymes.

I never thought to tell you then, as life got in the way,
And now the busy times have gone
I've thought of things I'd say . . . .
Like: Thank you just for being there when life was tough to
bare,
Especially times when I was ill, you always would be there.

I always meant to tell you,
But time got in the way . . . . .
But I promise that I'll tell you when we meet again . . .
            some day.

Before the storm.

Before the storm, all was still
The clouds were gathering over the hill.
The heavy sky was all foreboding,
Almost ready for unloading.

And then the wind began to stir,
In Alder, Oak, Ash and Fir.
Their branches all began to sway
With leaves all fluttering down the way.

A flash of lightening way up high,
Sent its tendrils spreading throughout the sky.
And then, one almighty 'crash'
Whilst more lightning began to 'flash'.

The angry clouds unleashed their grief
And their teardrops fell on every leaf.
Until the rain was lashing down
And hailstones bounced upon the ground.

The awesome sky now changed to blue
And then the sun came shining through,
And as I walked back down the lane . . .
Everything was fresh, there was peace again.

Just a face in the crowd.

A London street, the day is cold.
He sits there begging, he is cold.
His coat is ragged, his beard is grey,
The rain beats down for another day.
He's hungry, in a London street, now . . .
But nobody cares, they don't know how.
They throw some money in his bowl,
And someone is heard to say "Poor soul".
This could well be them some day,
But they are quickly on their way,
To houses which are dry and warm,
Their clothes are not old and torn.
In a London street, people are happy,
Busy and loud,
To them, he is . . . just a face in the crowd.
And I am very ashamed to say . . .
I was one in the crowd who walked away.

If Only.

'If only' we could turn back time,
Where days were carefree and sublime.
When we could dance and jump and run,
And every day was full of fun.
When energy was endless
And days were worry free.
Belongings never mattered,
We were happy as could be.
'If only' we were young again
Without enduring aches and pains.
With roller skates and skipping ropes,
And life before us full of hopes.
If we could step into the past,
And 'fix it' so that time could last
Where laughter would outweigh the tears
And we could conquer all our fears.
'If only' we had spent more time
With those we loved so dear,
And said the things we never said
Whilst they were there to hear.
Instead, we kept those words inside,
To fester and cause pain,
Today we wish we'd spilled them out
Then we'd be free again.
Today, we look back over time,
To things we've done and seen,
And wonder where the years have gone
That went by in between.
'If only' is a saying often used
When things we've done go wrong.
So could we change those words around to ;
'Only if' .... only if we're strong.

When all the fun stopped ('Fun Fair')

I hear the shrieks of laughter
As the 'dodgem' cars go by,
Their echoes fill this silent place
But now, they rust and die.
The 'Ferris' wheel no longer turns to shock the crowd below . .
There are no crowds, there is no show.

No 'Hot Dog' vendor at this agenda,
No 'neon' lights, no brawls, no fights.
No candy floss, no ice cream
The past has faded to a dream.
This was an exciting place to be in days of long ago,
But here it is, neglected now . . . there is no show.

No 'peep' shows, no puppets and no crowd,
Just the sound of silence, but, in my head, it's loud.

Sleep Walk.

Reflections in a rainy street,
You try to walk quietly with noisy feet.
Your heart is pounding as you hurry along,
The rain keeps falling but you must carry on.
You look around you with every stride,
You think you see shadows,
You just want to hide.

Every step that you take
Seems harder to make,
It feels as if someone has put on the brake.
Then, suddenly someone you know calls your name,
The relief that you feel is hard to explain.
But just as you're telling them how it has been . . .
All of a sudden . . . You wake up from your dream !

Following the Plough.

The farmer walks behind the plough,
His horses trudge uneven ground.
The blades cut deep within the sod,
With regimental furrows, deepest brown.

The seagulls follow knowingly,
Opportunists, with their squawking sound.
Rich soil indeed to plant the seed,
Crisp air and morning mists abound.

Farmer with flat cap of tweed, waistcoat and braces,
Jacket with neck-scarf, hob nailed boots and laces.
Trudging all day with sweat on his brow,
Leading his horses and following the plough.

Horses and man working as one,
Toiling through dark heavy soil in the sun.
Swishing of tails and flicking of manes,
Clinking horse brasses and jingling chains.

From dawn until dusk until your body is sore,
And you feel that you cannot endure any more.
Mile after mile to be done whilst you're able . . . . . .
And all this just to put food on the table.

Stitches of Patience.

Rainy days, when I would sit and watch
Whilst my Mum and Nan would be quietly sewing.
I learned so much from them whilst I was growing.

Simple pastimes, things made
With loving care and concentration
Now handed down from the last generation.

Every strand of silk guided through the eye of a needle
With anticipation!
A picture on cotton cloth with coloured variation.
Which would grow into a treasured creation.

Petals on flowers, made with delicate loops and knots,
All perfected with imagination.
I still have some of these treasures of a past time
When items that one made,
Were accepted with appreciation,
Quiet time, time when there was more communication.

Time has passed, and life has become fast
And there is no time . . . . . . no time
To share quiet times of contemplation.

But, I experienced something of a magical fascination,
Just through learning a pastime . . .
With 'one to one' special attention and dedication.

The Button Tin.

Some things in life are precious, my button tin is one,
It was my Grandma's long ago and it gave me so much fun.
I'd spread the buttons on the rug as I sat beside the fire,
And sort them into patterns for everyone to admire.

There were so many different kinds, I'd place them all in rows,
Each one would be examined and my love for them would
grow.
Each button had a story of where its life began . . .
An army coat, a skirt, a dress, a favourite cardigan.

Not only where there buttons, but press-studs, brooches too,
A rug hook and a pen knife, and laces for a shoe.

My childhood was so special, though it was not rich or grand
Many things were handed down and most were made by hand.
'Make do and mend' was common then, in those days so long ago
And nothing was impossible if you could knit or sew.

I've often thought as time goes by that simple things are best,
And when I see what folks have now, I don't feel too impressed.
Our world is full of 'mass produced' once used, then thrown
away,
With not enough recycled, or 'saved for a rainy day'.

I've seen the fashions come and go as years have slipped away,
'Vintage' has become the 'in' thing once more,
Sewing and knitting are back to stay!
I still have my Button Tin, it's dented, and as old as me,
Its contents remind me still
. . . . . . .of how things used to be.

SAT-NAV Insanity

We bought ourselves a Sat-Nav, a year or two ago,
To help us ease our journeys as we travelled to and fro.
We thought it would be easy just to pop the postcode in,
And take the strain off traveling with the map beneath my chin.

Never did I realise the trouble it would be,
As my spouse continually argued with a voice and not with me!
Our journeys took us longer than the'd ever done before,
And our nerves were often shattered before we'd set foot outside the door!

At times when we most needed some vital information,
The Sat-Nav would just shut off, as if to cause us more frustration!
It took us down some lonely roads, rirght off the beaten track
And we often wondered, as we strayed, if we'd ever make it back!

'Turn left at the next junction,' the same old voice would say,
Then we'd drive for several miles and often lose our way.
We'd often end up going in the opposite direction,
And decided that the MAP would be much easier on reflection!

We've been down roads near us we never knew existed,
And, if we knew what we know now, we know we'd have resisted.
(Now, there's a tongue twister!)

Oh! Bring back those days when journeys would be thoroughly enjoyed,
Before we'd spend good money on gadgets which turned out to be devoid.

At last, just when you know you're nearly home,
And you feel that jubilation,
Some smart-arse smug recording says:
'You've reached your destination!'

Winter's Cold Embrace.

When berries, shiny red adorn the trees,
And icy winds make ponds and puddles freeze.
When wearing Winter woollies make us feel so cosy,
And Winter breezes make our cheeks all rosy.

When logs are stacked against an old brick wall,
To bring a bright warm fireside to us all.
When frosty mornings bring on a festive feeling,
And decorations fill a once bare ceiling.

When church bells chime and choirs begin to sing,
And Christmas trees are dressed with all their 'bling'.
When ploughed up fields replace the Summer corn,
And a frosty sunrise greets a winter dawn.

When 'crispy' Autumn leaves have all but gone,
Revealing stark silhouettes against the fading sun.
Then, as Winter sheds its cold embrace . . . . .
Another Spring will quietly take its place.

Cottage by the Sea

A tiny cottage by the sea
How wonderful the views would be.
Oh! I could sit for hours and more
Just watching waves that lap the shore.
With fluffy clouds in bright blue skies
And sailing boats, and sea birds' cries.
And even when the days were grey
I'd sit and while the hours away
All tucked up safely in the warm
To watch the wonder of a storm.
And when the days were over
And the moon shone on the sea,
And the twinkling stars blinked all around,
How magical that would be!!

All in a Heart Beat.

Complete peace, it's a thing that does exist,
In an empty place,
Where just your footsteps
And your heart beat can be heard.

Silence, that free feeling
Which echoes through your very being
In a place where many have come and gone.

This is the peaceful place
Where you can feel 'their' existence.
Your own existence is pending . . . .
All in a heart beat.

Echoes on the stairway.

The paintwork, all flaked and old,
The damp is seeping through.
The banisters are rotting
Where the wood's become wet through.
But think of how it used to be
So elegant and grand,
With people passing up and down,
Some, maybe hand in hand.
But time has gone and things decay
As years go by so fast.
But stand and listen and you'll hear the echoes of the past.

Hopes and Dreams.

There is a special place somewhere,
Tucked away from view.
The sort of place I'd like to be,
To spend my whole life through.
I may not find it straight away,
As dreams are far and few.
But if I ever find that place,
I hope I'll be with you.

Streets Walls and Secrets.

How many feet have trodden these streets
In olden times and new?
How many hopes and dreams,
And how many have come true?
Old cobbled streets and ancient walls,
They hold their secrets well.
We shall never know my friends . . .
And 'they' will never tell.

Promise of Life

Through frost and snow, in wind and rain,
The flowers all will bloom again.
Don't give up in times of woe,
When things go wrong and you are low.
Time will heal as life goes by
And just as flowers fade and die,
You too, will come to life once more . . . .
The flowers will bloom, just like before.

When the Tide comes rolling in.

When the tide comes rolling in, be it gentle or roaring,
Rippling over rocks to and fro in endless momentum
Along with the beat of my heart.
It mesmerises and astounds me, how gentle it can be,
But then, another time, a frightening place to be.

When the tide comes rolling in, it brings with it
The flotsam and jetsam for me to explore, to observe,
As the sand shifts beneath my feet,
And the wind caresses my face.

When the tide comes rolling in . . . .
I am the humble spectator of all natures beauty.

The Weight Watcher.

I was standing in the bathroom, looking at my figure,
And I thought, "Oh blimey, you'll have to slim
Before you get much bigger"
So I threw out all my mirrors, so I wouldn't see myself,
And I put my bowl of sugar on my very highest shelf.

Every time I passed a sweet shop, I looked the other way,
And thought of all the times I'd had a Mars bar every day!
I started buying slimming food, crisp breads and all that
racket,
But after tasting what they were like, I'd have sooner eaten
the packet!

When I was in a dress shop, I'd pace about the floor,
The shop assistant would smugly say, "Size 18 you're looking
for?"
So I joined a keep fit class, to keep me nice and trim
But I ached in every muscle, so I had to jack it in!

I'll stop at nothing this year to get into my bikini,
But getting myself out of it will be likened to Houdini!
I'm fed up with seeing bulges every time I get undressed
I threw away my bathroom scales because I got depressed!

So I'm counting up my calories and making sacrifices,
I've given up my cream cakes, biscuits and choc-ices.
But wait till Summer's over, and Winter winds do blow,
I'll throw away the sweeteners . . . .
And back to 'pudds' I'll go!

The Sea-shore.

The seagulls hovered high above as I stood there on the shore.
I remembered happy childhood days I'd spent there years before.
Building castles in the sand and jumping over waves
Collecting shells and pebbles, exploring rocks and caves.

Then I became a woman and had children of my own
And I watched them do the self-same things . . . . .
Oh! How those years have flown.

Our life seems like the sea-shore, it changes constantly,
The years are like the shifting sand and restless like the sea.
Our troubles are like stormy seas which dash against the shore,
Our happiness, sand castles and fluffy clouds galore.

The rocks we climb are challenges we face from day to day
And the shells collected are the friends we make . . . . .
As we travel upon life's way.

The Mask I wear.

Nobody knows just how I feel.
I may be false, I may be real.
The mask I wear hides all my tears,
It hides my thoughts, it hides my fears.

Nobody knows the pain inside,
The mask is there, I laugh, I hide.
My friends may think that all is well,
But they don't know, they just can't tell.

My mask conceals what lies within,
The tears well up, I keep them in.
I know I must not show alarm,
The mask will show that I am calm.

They think I have no worries,
They cannot really see.
I wear my mask so skilfully,
They know not who is me.

I show concern for others,
I cheer them on their way.
"Don't worry, it's not as bad
As it may seem," I say.

But I know what I'm hiding,
And no one else can see.
My mask is switched to 'cheerful'
And they know that face is me.

Who knows what's real and what is fake?
What lies are told, what risks we take?
Who knows what others really feel . . .
And if they're false, or if they're real?
The thing is, we can never tell,
If others wear a mask as well.
We may be on life's massive stage,
All acting out our masquerades.

One day my mask will be removed and everyone will see,
The person who is really there . . . . . .
The person who is ME.

The Lonely Road.

The road stretched out before me,
It looked so hard and long.
I glanced back where I'd come from
And prayed that I'd be strong.

Every step I trod was difficult,
Slow motion in my mind.
Where would my journey take me
What adventure would I find?

The road of life is hard and long
We take turnings all the way.
The challenges are hills we climb,
We make decisions every day.

Some journeys never seem to end
When every road has one more bend.
But when you find the going tough
And every surface hard and rough . . . .

Remember just how far you've come
Rejoice! Take pride in what you've done!

Dry Stone Wall.

Stone by stone, all laid by hand,
Creating walls throughout the land.
Barriers laid with patience and skill,
By generations who are doing it still.

Lay your stones carefully, one by one,
Be mindful of balancing them as they come.
Balance one wrong and the whole lot could fall,
Spoiling the beauty of your dry stone wall.

We have to balance the 'stones' of our days,
Be mindful of tones in our words and our ways.
Once we have laid our foundations with care,
The rest will fit nicely and not need repair.
So build your stones wisely and you will soon see,
The wonderful completion, of your legacy.

Simple Deeds.

I'm not the sort who needs a lot of thanks for what I do,
I do it because I love to, and it makes me feel good too!
For if we can help somebody as we pass along life's path
And have a little 'chatter' and make somebody laugh,
Then we have done a special thing
Which never could be bought
Just by doing something simple
Without giving it a thought.
We've lifted them when they were low
And lifted ourselves too,
We've spent no money in the process,
And not even thought it through.

A favour doesn't always need a favour in return,
And folks who seek for gratitude have such a lot to learn.
Just a smile can make a difference
Even when we're feeling sad,
And if that person smiles right back
It makes us more than glad!

So if you want to help someone
Just DO IT, for the pleasure,
And leave a legacy that says
You were one of life's pure treasures!

The dreaded 'Take Away'. (Not for the faint hearted!)

I never had the urge for one, I couldn't be persuaded,
I always said I'd never let my stomach be invaded.
But then, before I'd had the chance to say "I'd rather not"
Someone went and ordered it and I fell for the plot!

It didn't smell too bad (I thought) so I tucked in like a mate,
And now, the morning after, I'm afraid it is too late.
I'm sitting on the toilet, (and I'm sure you feel for me)
As I'm feeling rather poorly and as weak as I can be.

I knew I should have left it where
All 'Take-a-ways' belong,
But friendships mean a lot to me, and
My will power's not too strong.
I said I was 'allergic', but they didn't understand,
And then, after I'd had a drink, things got slightly out of hand!

What I wanted was a Pizza, but that wasn't on the list,
And all the other options look quite 'fuzzy' when you're pissed!
And then, all eyes upon me, I indulged with sudden haste,
I didn't want my friends to know I didn't like the taste.

I wonder where those friends are now??
The friends that I respected,
Whilst I am sitting here all alone
And feeling all rejected.

As now, 12 hours later I sit here looking glum,
I have to take the 'punishment' and this seat's hard on my bum.
If I could turn the clock back, I'd definitely say "NO"
As last nights bloody curry has left me all aglow!!!

When somebody Cares.

Isn't it just wonderful when somebody is there?
Just being close to comfort you, someone who'll really care.
Just when you're at rock bottom,
When you feel you can't go on,
That 'someone' lifts you up on high
And tries to make you strong.
That's when you know the feeling that someone really cares
They'll go the extra mile for you, they'll wipe away those tears.
You'll feel that life's worth living, you'll feel you 'can' go on.
So if you ever need someone . . . I hope I'll be that 'one'!

When the Piano ceased to Play.

I can still hear the notes that were played on these keys,
But now they are silent, along with the dust and cobwebs of age.
Its music lost in time, along with the pianist
Who lovingly caressed the ebony and ivory
Making it sing up and down the scales.
Music books, with their lines of crotchets and quavers,
Now yellow with time, lay in piles, their pages
Never to be turned between notes.
No longer do the audience cry out for 'more'
The audience is long gone.
Just the memories linger, of crescendos, bow ties,
Tuxedos and cigarette smoke curling into the air,
Spiralling upward along with the music
Of times gone by.

Shopping Mall.

Futuristic places.
Shop windows, models with no faces.
Fancy neon lighting, steel and glass,
Beckoning you into the materialistic farce.
Piped music and escalators,
Buskers entertaining spectators.
False fabric, cheap, but not cheap clothes
Hanging in rows and rows.
Made by people who don't have a choice . . .
People without a voice.

I seem alone in the crowd
Everything is magnified and loud.
People buying things they don't really need,
Paying with 'plastic' caught up in a world of greed.
Futuristic places . . .
Engulfing all our green spaces.

It's all in my mind.

The old cottage still stands the way I knew it years ago,
Within the brickwork, cracks begin to show.
Roof tiles with bright orange lichen,
And tufts of moss so green,
And holes in masonry where bees have been.
Wisteria has engulfed the tired walls,
Cascading its tales of petals like waterfalls.
A blaze of scented flowers line
The cobbled path up to the door,
In all this world, one could not ask for more.
Around the door, the roses invite you with a smile,
With fragrant bowers beckoning all the while.
Past generations have formed this cosy place,
Embellishing its nooks and crannies
With pretty cushions and curtains of lace.
Simplicities in life are all around,
If you look hard enough, they can be found.
And if you cannot find them, close your eyes,
Imagine you are there . . . .
Our minds are more amazing than we could ever be aware!

Dance of the Swallows.

They're here again! Oh how they grace the sky,
With acrobatic dips and dives displayed on high.
With a 'screech' and a 'twit' as they swoop to and fro,
Catching tiny insects as they go.
Every year in Spring they bring us such delight,
With such energy and agility after their long flight.
Twisting and turning overhead with ease,
On these sunny days upon the pleasant breeze.
Overwhelming us, intriguing us on high . . . . .
The Swallows dance, and their stage is the eternal sky.

I heard an Organ play.

I stood in peace, no one was there,
The sun shone bright, though cool, the air.
The dusty church was cold and bare.
But as I stood and looked around
I thought I heard a distant sound,
And then I turned to walk away . . .
That's when I heard an organ play.
I wonder, could it be a sign?
No, . . just the echoes of a distant time.

Which way do you hang your Toilet Roll?
(A true story, but not for the squeamish!)

When I was just a little soul,
We never used a toilet roll.
Back then, things were pretty sparse,
With newspaper to wipe your arse!

We'd cut it into nice neat squares
And thread it on some string.
With the lack of sewage systems back then,
This was the normal thing.

We'd sit upon the wooden seat,
With galvanised bucket tucked beneath,
It was a natural thing to us,
And so, we never made a fuss.

A trench was dug strategically,
Somewhere out of sight,
And the bucket would be emptied
In the very dead of night!

We never had to buy manure,
We had our own supply,
No problem growing vegetables,
They flourished low and high!

On Summer days when it was hot,
You wouldn't hang about a lot!
As flies would gather round about,
So you'd shut the door, and just GET OUT!
When Winter came, and days were cold,
You'd put it off . . . and try to 'hold'!
You wouldn't want to sit there long . . .
Unless you had a blanket on!

One thing which was a Godsend,
You never had to queue,
As nobody was that keen
To stay long in 'THAT' loo!

All this (my avid reader)
Must seem quite primitive,
But in those bygone days back then,
That's how we used to live.

There never was a 'chain' or 'handle'
To flush the waste away,
We never had the luxuries
That folks all have today.

Now, we have 'posh' toilet rolls
Of several 'ply' and more!
No newspaper cut in squares
And hung behind the toilet door!

People now will never know,
The hardships we had long ago.
I thank my lucky stars today,
That we don't have to live that way.

So ... when you go to wipe your BUM,
Just think how lucky we've become,
To actually have the time to plan,
Which way the toilet roll should HANG!

Nothing in Life is for Certain.

She sat with a shawl around her shoulders,
She looked straight ahead with a smile.
Her hands, placed in lap were all wrinkled,
The nurse tended her nails with a file.
Those hands which had once been so active,
And created so many good things.
Now, the vivid veins stood out like grey rivers,
Her fingers too small for her rings.
Her thick dark hair, which once was her glory,
Was now white as snow and so thin.
Her eyes which were once bright and fiery,
Now were bloodshot and looking quite grim.
Her character, once outgoing and witty,
Was now very quiet and withdrawn.

The strong body, which once gave me life in this world
Was now very frail and forlorn.
I took a long look at my Mother,
And I thought back to how she had been.
And I felt the tears 'well up' inside me,
At the illness and sadness she'd seen.
Nothing in life is for 'Certain',
We can never foretell what's ahead,
For no matter what we are expecting,
Something else may just turn up instead.
Our bodies will not last forever,
The ageing process can be so cruel,
We are privileged, but don't always know it,
All the while we have plenty of fuel.
So do what you can whilst you're able,
And thank God above every day,
Because ONE thing in life IS for 'Certain' . . . . . .
We are all heading the same way.

Live in Hope.

I've never set my 'hopes' too high,
But I'm always optimistic.
I don't need disappointment,
But must be realistic.
As things are hard to come by,
You have to work it through.
Persevere persistently with all you ever do.

There will be times when days are hard
And nothing seems to gel,
When everything you touch goes wrong
And you go through 'merry hell'.
That's the time you must be strong
And take it on the chin.
Keep 'plugging' through your problems step by step
And watch it all fit in.

There's a saying, "Things are never as bad as they may seem."
And if you don't 'hope' for something,
You'll never achieve your dream.
There's also a saying "Live in hope," and that I've always done.
Without it, I'd not be the woman I've become.
So live off of positivity and you will find one day,
Your prospects may be brighter, in a weird and wondrous way!

Train Ride.

Oh! The excitement of catching a train
The waiting on platforms again and again.
Seeing that 'giant' come puffing along,
Chuffing and panting and whistling its song.
Oh! How my heart would just melt at the sight
As the steam would 'belch' out, with all of its might.
The carriages, all wooden and polished with care,
The black soot that lingered (sometimes in your hair!)
You'd hang your head out of the window at times,
To wave at the workmen as they stood by the lines.
The smell of those steam trains still lingers with me,
And the memories of family who I went to see.
Memories now, they await renovation,
One day they will carry a new generation.

I'm Nobody's Fool.

When I was young and timid, and shy as I could be,
Experience was lacking, and kids all bullied me.
I dreaded school because I knew
That I'd be teased and scorned,
And so I played at being sick and
Stayed home all forlorn.
But staying home would never help
Me conquer all my fears,
So I faced them with a grimace,
And I smiled right through those tears.

As life went by, I made good friends,
And so life changed for me,
I realized where I'd gone wrong,
Gained confidence, felt free.
Free from being ridiculed for everything I'd said,
And happy I could stand up proud,
After all those tears I'd shed.

Now I look back at all the years, and things that I have done,
And feel very elated that my battle has been won.
I've dealt with all those challenges
That life has thrown my way,
And gone through very painful times,
When I could hardly bear each day.

All that has made me stronger
From those far off days at school.
Now I can take on anything . . . . .
Because, I'm nobody's fool.

I know I've put it somewhere.

I'm feeling so frustrated, I'm hot and bothered too.
I know I've put it somewhere and I'm not sure what to do.
I've looked in all those places where I thought that it might be,
The only one who knows it's location, unfortunately is me!

I've searched all through my handbag,
And hunted high and low,
I know I've put it somewhere,
But only I would know!
So it's no good asking someone else,
They wouldn't have a clue,
They'd look with their raised eyebrows saying:
"That's a silly thing to do"

I've hunted in my cupboards,
And looked all through my drawers,
(And I know it's not a pretty sight,
But I've been down on all fours!)
I remember even saying that it would be safer 'there' . . .
And now I know it must have been,
As I can't remember where!

I should have put it somewhere
Where I knew where I could find it,
A place which would be obvious,
And then I wouldn't mind it.
But no! I had to put it in a place where I'd forget,
So now I'm sweating buckets, and in a proper fret.

I know I've put it somewhere, but I can't look any more . . .
(The truth is, I've forgotten, just what I'm looking for!)

Away from it all.

A quiet place is what I seek,
Away from city, town and street.
A place where I can sit and dream,
Perhaps beside a glittering stream.
Where shadows dance between the trees,
Whilst leaves all rustle in the breeze.
A place where I can think and write,
A mossy place dappled with light.
Where verse comes easy to my mind,
I can relax and unwind.

It could be on a hilltop high,
Where mists abound and eagles fly.
Where clouds hang in mauve mountain heights
And sunbeams shed their streaks of light . . . (where
imagination can take flight!)

It could be on a beach somewhere,
With fluffy clouds and sea-fresh air.
Where gentle waves caress the shore,
With shells and pebbles to explore.

I don't mind the weather, bright or bleak,
A quiet place is what I seek.
And when I find that magic place,
I'll store it in my mind . . .
As quiet places these days,
Are very hard to find!

The 'Wind' of change!

Here I stand, all alone, I 'farted' in a fresh air zone.
Everybody walked away, they didn't really want to stay!
Rejected now and all deflated, 'twas more than I anticipated!

My flatulence, as I've grown older, is uncontrolled and
somewhat bolder.
I try and slip into a crowd, so know one hears if it is loud!
My confidence has been diminished, my social life is all but
finished.
But I must go on without remorse, as nature always takes it's
course.
I'm positive, I have not sinned . . . .
There is no guilt in passing wind!

A Photograph of Grandma.

I keep it in a silver frame, it's of a bygone age.
From days when photography was at an early stage.
She's standing very straight and still, beside an upright chair,
She's looking to the camera with a distant, serious stare.
Her face is very beautiful, with skin so soft and pure,
Her brown hair piled up high on top and looking quite demure.
She wore a pure white blouse that day with dainty frills and lace,
She seemed to have a 'presence' of innocence and grace.
I often take a look at her and think how things were then.
A world completely different, for women, and for men.
When work was hard and money short, and things all changing fast.
She must have had her hopes and fears in that picture of the past.
I often sat and talked to her when she was old and grey,
And I wish I'd asked her more about her life back in those days.
'If only' is a phrase we often use, when we regret,
The times we had a chance to say things, and then tend to forget.
She's an ancestor I'm proud of, and I loved her company,
And when I stood beside her grave, it flooded back to me.
Just a 'click' of a camera shutter, and she's captured for all time.
A memory in a photograph, to be kept for me, and mine.

Carousel

The Carousel goes round and round,
The horses all go up and down.
The music makes a welcome sound
Whilst people gather all around.
The painted wood, the coloured lights
They make the ride a sheer delight.

Our lives are like the Carousel
We're happy most when all is well.
But sometimes there are ups and downs
When our whole life is whirling round.
We have to bear the rise and fall
And face the music through it all.

The painted days when sun shines through,
When we can see things all anew.
The fairground organ's happy tune
Lifts sombre thoughts away quite soon.

So try and see the brighter side
Of ups and downs upon life's ride
And then you'll find that all is well . . . .
Whilst riding your own Carousel !

Chasing Shadows

When I was young, I'd often chase my shadow just for fun.
But I'd never ever catch it, however fast I'd run!
I'd watch it sideways-on as I was walking down the street,
And see if it would disappear when I quickly took a peep!
But no! It always followed me wherever I would go,
That is, as long as Mr. Sun would watch me come and go!
I'd hop and jump, go backwards, and it still would follow me.
It was there when I was skipping, or when I'd climb a tree.
But every time the sun went in, I'd sadly stop and stare,
As all the places I would search, my shadow wasn't there.
I'd frantically look up and down, and all around that place.
I'd miss that shadow . . . I had no one else to chase.
As life went by, I saw that there were shadows everywhere,
As long as lovely Mr. Sun would shine and put them there!
The clouds would cast their shadows as they floated in the sky,
They made a Summer day so bright as they hung up there so high.
On rainy days I'd be indoors and miss its bright warm rays,
I'd long for it to shine again and enjoy those happy days.
When I grew older, I found out that shadows gently fall,
As Mr. Sun fades far from sight, and disappears from all.
I've learnt so much as time has past and sunshine comes and goes,
And dark clouds cast their shadows,
As the cold wind howls and blows.
But we can spread our own sunshine, no matter what the weather,
With just a smile and cheery word to bring the world together!
If we're always chasing shadows, we never see the sun,
There's a little bit of sunshine to find in everyone.
But you have to search to find it, as it's often hidden deep,
They've always seen the shadows when behind the sun they creep.
If you always see the sunshine, but never see the rain
You'll never know what others feel who often suffer pain.

So be somebody's rainbow who appears after a storm
And fill their days with sunshine to make their heart feel warm.
Shine your little light out there when days feel dull and grim,
Bring that happiness to everyone, feel that 'glimmer' deep within!

A Picture Painted in Words.

If I could paint a picture, and mix the colours right,
I'd capture early sun and mist, and evening's shadowed light.
I'd revel in its beauty at the brush strokes as they flowed,
And I'd glory in emerging scenes, and colours as they glowed.

There'd be thatched cottages so sweet,
With rambling roses over doors.
Hills and mountains in the distance,
And in the foreground, heather on moors.

Rippling streams, rocky water falls
And reflections in a pond,
And bright blue skies with fluffy clouds
Into the far beyond.

With fields of green and glistening seas
And trees all swaying in the breeze.
I'd capture them with loving care
To fill a canvas previously bare.

But when I try to paint those scenes, they never go to plan.
The artist finds it easy, but me, I never can.
My note pad is my canvas, and my pen shall be my brush.
I'll write the picture carefully as there is no need to rush.
The thoughts and 'words' come easily
As they flow into a rhyme,
And the picture locked inside my mind
Shall be written for all time.

The Legacy in the Leaves.

How beautiful the leaves as they grow old.
They keep their colour, bright and bold.
And then, at last they shrivel and die,
They fall to earth to fade with a sigh.
But in dying, they will feed the earth
And give small saplings chance of birth.

As we grow older, we could be
The same as leaves upon the tree.
Fading gracefully with age
As each day we turn another page.
Spreading colour every day
In all we do and all we say.

And then, at last our turn will come
To part this life when all is done.
But we shall be just like the tree . . . .
Each leaving to others, our legacy.

At Life's Helm.

My boat is in the harbour, the weather's set for fair.
Don't know my destination yet, and not sure that I care.
I've sailed through stormy seas before, and always reached the shore
But cannot be so certain I'll achieve it any more.
My body is much older now and cannot stand the strain.
The challenges are harder and the journey causes pain.
When skies are blue and waters calm, the going can be fine,
But stormy skies and restless seas destroy a boat like mine.
I'm not sure that I'm ready and the time is running out,
Should I take the chance and go ahead, or stay here full of doubt?
Only I can have the final word on when my boat sets sail,
But who can say what dangers lurk and whether I will fail?
Our 'hulls' are full of good intent, and our 'compass' set in line,
Our 'rudder' keeps us steady on our journey throughout time.
Our lives are full of challenges, they 'anchor' us off shore,
They make us doubt our abilities to 'set our sails' once more.
But we'll all find our resting place in a 'harbour' full of calm,
Where the waves no longer lash our 'boughs'
And place our boats in harm.
Our weary 'hulls' can rest at last,
And we'll tie our ropes up hard and fast.
With life's restless sea behind us, with it's shifting raging foam,
Our pain will be a distant storm,
No doubts, no fears . . . . .
In a peaceful place called 'home'.

Winter's Angels. (The Snowdrop.)

Angels of Winter, here you are again,
In all your delicate glory.
Your shy nodding heads of pure white,
And perfectly formed petals, showing small frilly under-skirts.

You have forced your way up through frosted ground
Once more to greet us, from a cold dark place in the earth.
To brave yet another season of icy winds.

From a tiny bulb, which we thought,
Might have rotted in relentless downpours.
But no, you have survived yet another winter.
Brave white Angels, giving us pure pleasure to behold.
Hope . . . . for another Springtime to come.

Ted's Beloved Greenhouse

Old Ted, he loved his garden, it was his pride and joy.
He'd always liked to see things growing since he was a boy.
His vegetables were the envy of everyone in sight,
Especially his neighbour Bill (because his had caught the blight!)

But Ted was not preturbed by this, (what's more, he didn't care!)
As last year he'd won the trophy at the horticultural fare.
No matter what Ted planted, it never failed to grow
Fruit trees, shrubs and vegetables, they flourished high and low.

Now, one day Ted decided that a greenhouse was a 'must'
He drew out substantial savings and invested it with lust!
Once it was erected, he stood back with pure delight,
Now old Ted could potter there from early morn until night.
Pricking out his tiny seeds and nurturing his marrows,
Tending his tomatoes he would while away the hours.
He'd never been so happy, (and neither had his wife,)
Because at last she'd get some peace for the first time in her life!!

Alas! One morning Ted awoke to see a sight which made him sick . . . .
Through his beloved greenhouse, someone had 'lobbed' a brick!!
His leaf mould and his compost were strewn across the floor,
His grow-bags had been disembowelled , and his marrows grew no
more!

All his work was ruined and gone, this was far too much for Ted.
He had a confrontation with his neighbour Bill, and some tears were
shed.
Ted claimed for compensation for the damage and the stress
And Bill was so embarrassed that he'd had to confess.

No longer will you find Ted in his garden or his shed . . .
He's been and bought a Classic car and he's playing with that instead!

Up on the Moors.

Up on the moors where the wind blows so cold,
The landscape is rugged, craggy and bold.
Up with your collar and quicken your pace,
As the freezing cold blizzard stings hard on your face.

Your rucksack is heavy with all of your gear
And the sound of the weather is all that you hear.
The sheep go on 'munching' as you pass them by,
And the Eagle is watching you, way up in the sky.

Up on the Moors on a much different day,
When the sun is warm, the sky blue, not grey.
The landscape has colour, and the sound that you hear,
Is the call of the birds, a delight to your ear.

The Heather and Gorse is a joy to your eye,
And the Eagle's still up there, watching on high.
But today you can see all his wonderful feathers
As your eyes are not hampered with the 'wrath' of the weather.
So, off with your jacket as you catch the suns rays,
And thank the Lord up above for these happy warm days!

Only a Tree.

In ancient woodland here I stand,
Surveying all around me close at hand.
Bluebells and primroses at my feet,
And in my branches, birds do flit and tweet.
Within my bark the insects find a home,
And sometimes happy children climb me as they roam.

In Spring, my fresh green buds burst into sight,
In Summer, I have reached my full delight.
In Autumn, my leaves enrich the earth around,
And in Winter, my silhouette is stark and sound.

But as the seasons change and years pass by,
And my canopy grows closer to the sky,
I see a sight in distant fields ahead
Which fills me with a sudden awful dread.
As the chainsaws and the diggers all pursue,
This ancient wood will disappear from view.
To destroy us for another building site,
And the thought of this fills me and mine with fright.

No more will 'wild' things fly and roam,
No more will insects find a home.
Instead there will be cities, towns and roads,
As concrete mixers spread their heavy loads.

Tarmac will cover fields where Skylarks once took flight,
And MANS pollution will complete the eventual blight.
Humans who cared about our plight
Put up banners, fought the fight,
But all this fell upon deaf ears....
As it has done for years and years.

So, here I stand in ancient woodland ... only a tree
But mankind MUST learn, that HE cannot exist
Without the likes of ME.......

The 'one' who holds the moon.

Every waterfall that flows.
Every blade of grass that grows.
Every leaf on every tree,
The 'one' who holds the moon can see.

Every bird that sings its tune.
Every flower's sweet perfume.
Every river, every stream.
Every sunset's fading beam.
Each wave that folds with ebb and flow,
The 'one' who holds the moon will know.

The seasons as they come and go,
The Summer heat, the Winter snow.
Every storm and every tide,
The moon takes charge of how they ride.

Everyone who goes astray.
Everyone who kneels to pray.
Every soul that feels forsaken.
Every breath that's ever taken.
Someone's there to see it all,
With every rise and every fall.

Each broken heart for one who's gone,
The ones who're left who must be strong
To brace themselves and carry on . . .
They will not go unheard for long.

Everyone who values earth
Appreciates how much it's worth.
But those who's greed is beyond care,
They'll never even be aware
That the 'one' who holds the moon is there.

The 'one' who holds the moon controls
The transportation of our souls.
So, whatever road we choose to take
Whatever rules we tend to break,
Whatever comes, whatever goes
The 'one' who holds the moon . . .
'HE' knows.

About the Author

Anne was born in the county of Kent in England in 1946. She and her parents lived with her grandmother in an old terraced house until she was eight years old when her father, who then worked on the railway, acquired a railway house.

Anne grew up during an age of 'make do and mend' after the war and was influenced in hand writing by her grandmother before starting school. She always loved putting 'words' together, but never started writing poetry until the 1960s, often by observing people and compiling something humorous.

Anne has always possessed a mischievous streak, and that comes across in some of her work, but she also has a more serious, deep side as she writes about the past, present, and experiences of her own life.

She is passionate about the environment and conservation. She still lives in Kent with her husband and has a son and daughter and three grown up grandchildren.

Lightning Source UK Ltd.
Milton Keynes UK
UKHW051230201220
375447UK00015B/1879